INDIGENOUS AMERICAN CULTURES

Celebrating the SIOUX

ANNE ACCARDI

Mitchell Lane
PUBLISHERS

Parent and Caregiver Tips for Creating Nonfiction Readers

The high-interest topics in the ***Indigenous American Cultures*** series are sure to get your young reader excited about reading nonfiction. While exploring a fascinating subject, your reader will be introduced to new facts, ideas, and vocabulary.

Tips for Reading Nonfiction

Talk about Nonfiction

Explain that nonfiction books provide facts about real-world topics. When readers read nonfiction, they gain a rich understanding of the world. They build background knowledge that provides a foundation for learning and academic success.

Look at the Parts

This book contains the following helpful features. Share the purpose of each feature with your reader.

Photos, Captions, and Graphic Aids
The photos, captions, maps, diagrams, time lines, and other graphic aids in nonfiction texts contain a wealth of information. Help your reader identify different ways information can be displayed.

Sidebars
These extra tidbits of information help satisfy readers' curiosity and expand their knowledge.

Table of Contents
Located at the front of the book, this list shows the big ideas within the text and the page numbers where they can be found.

Glossary
Located at the back of the book, the glossary defines key words and phrases that are related to the topic. These words and phrases can be found in the text in colored type.

Comprehension Questions (Fact Check)
Multiple-choice questions help readers self-check to make sure they understand what they read.

Index
Located at the back of the book, the index is an alphabetical list of topics and the page numbers where they can be found.

With a little help and guidance, your reader will be on their way to enjoying and learning from nonfiction books.

Mitchell Lane
PUBLISHERS
mitchelllanepub.com

2001 SW 31st Avenue
Hallandale, FL 33009

First Edition, 2026.
Author: Anne Accardi
Designer: Rhea Magaro
Editor: Kim Thompson

Series: Indigenous American Cultures
Title: Celebrating the Sioux / by Anne Accardi

Hallandale, FL : Mitchell Lane Publishers, [2026]

Library bound ISBN: 979-8-89260-556-4
Paperback ISBN: 979-8-89260-592-2
eBook ISBN: 979-8-89260-557-1

PHOTO CREDITS
Alamy: Maxim Ermolenko, cover, 1; PRISMA ARCHIVO, 6; Stania Kasula, 9; Yvette Cardozo, 17; The Protected Art Archive, 19; Danita Delimont, 25; Hemis, 25; Artography and Designs, 19; Public Domain: Wiki 7, 8, 18, 26, 27; Wiki/NARA, 9; Library of Congress, 12, 16; August Schwerdfeger, 21; Shutterstock: Michael Kaercher, cover, 1; Petr Podrouzek, cover, 1; Pierre Jean Durieu, cover, 1; JohnDSmith, 5; Cheri Alguire, 10; Tom Reichner, 11; Bettpix, 12; Jon Lauriat, 13; Steve Skjold, 14, 15; Janny2, 17; Pierre Jean Durieu, 18; Marian Weyo, 21; ThunderBirdEye, 22, 23; Jeffrey T. Kreulen, 24; Natursports, 27; Pierre Jean Durieu, 28; Jeffrey M. Frank, 29;

CONTENTS

A SIOUX CONNECTION

You have probably seen pictures of, or even visited, Mount Rushmore. At this monument in South Dakota, the faces of four United States presidents are carved into a mountainside in the Black Hills.

You may not know that the site is part of the homeland of the **Indigenous** Sioux people. They have lived in the area for thousands of years. To the Sioux, the Black Hills are **sacred**. They want the land returned to them.

Culture Close-Up

In 1980, the U.S. government offered to pay the Sioux 100 million dollars for the Black Hills, which the Sioux call *Paha Sapa*. The Sioux never took the money. They say that the special place is not for sale.

SIOUX HISTORY

At the time Europeans arrived in North America, the Sioux were one of the oldest and largest Indigenous groups on the continent. They lived across the Great Plains on land that is now North Dakota, South Dakota, Montana, Wyoming, Colorado, and Nebraska.

Long ago, the Sioux traveled from place to place to hunt bison. They were known as strong warriors and skilled hunters.

Culture Close-Up

The Great Sioux Nation is made up of three main groups: Lakota, Dakota, and Nakota. Each group has a number of individual tribes. The Sioux call themselves *Oceti Sakowin*, which means "Seven Council Fires."

Sitting Bull

In 1874, gold was discovered in the Black Hills. White **settlers** wanted Sioux land. Sioux leaders such as Crazy Horse and Sitting Bull led battles against U.S. soldiers. In the end, the Sioux were defeated. They were forced to move onto **reservations**.

Pine Ridge Reservation in 1890

Pine Ridge Reservation today

Today, there are about 160,000 Sioux people in the U.S. Many live on the Pine Ridge Reservation in South Dakota.

EXPLORING SIOUX PLACES

You can learn about the Sioux by visiting Wind Cave National Park in South Dakota. The Sioux believe that the first humans came from Wind Cave. People have explored the cave for many years, but no one has found the end yet!

The park is home to many bison. They are part of an effort to bring bison back to the Great Plains. Sioux groups are involved in bison **conservation**. The Rosebud Sioux Tribe has set aside tens of thousands of acres of grassland for bison. They have the largest Indigenous-owned bison herd in the world.

Culture Close-Up

Some people call bison "buffalo." Buffalo are native to Africa and Asia, while bison are found in North America and Europe. The two species are similar, but they are not the same. Long ago, millions of bison roamed the Great Plains. By 1900, fewer than 1,000 were left.

You can also visit the Crazy Horse Memorial in the Black Hills. Crazy Horse was a Lakota warrior who fought to protect Sioux lands. The courageous chief was killed by a U.S. soldier in 1877.

Crazy Horse led his people across the Great Plains after they were driven from their homes by the U.S. Army.

A giant sculpture of the leader is being carved into the face of a mountain. Crazy Horse's outstretched hand points toward Sioux homelands. The project began in 1948, and it is not yet complete.

Culture Close-Up

Crazy Horse led the warriors who defeated U.S. soldiers at the Battle of the Little Bighorn in 1876.

SIOUX LANGUAGES

The Lakota, Dakota, and Nakota each speak a different **dialect** in the Siouan language family. Today, few people speak these languages well. Not many people are left who learned the languages as children.

The Lakota Language Consortium is working to change this. In 2023, the organization released a new Lakota dictionary and a free app that helps people learn Lakota.

Culture Close-Up

Practice these Lakota words and phrases.

Hau. (Hello.)

Emáčiyapi (My name is)

Philámayaye. (Thank you.)

kȟolá (friend)

tȟatȟáŋka (bison)

HONORING SIOUX TRADITIONS

Long ago, the Sioux created things from natural materials. Blankets, clothing, and **tepees** were made from bison **hides**. Hides were painted with symbols and pictures to show hunts, battles, and prayers. Porcupine quills were dyed and woven into patterns to decorate clothing and moccasins. Later, glass beads replaced quills.

Today, Sioux artists continue the traditions. They use animal hides, beads, and symbols in their work. Some Sioux people wear traditional clothing when they attend festivals and ceremonies.

Culture Close-Up

Animals often appear in Sioux art. The Sioux think of animals as family members. Bison and horses hold a special place of honor. Eagles and eagle feathers symbolize strength and courage.

Music is important to the Sioux. Many of their songs are sacred. Musicians play drums, flutes, rattles, and whistles. They bring people together to sing, dance, and celebrate.

Culture Close-Up

Mato Wayuhi composes music for films and TV shows. The South Dakota artist is also an actor, singer, and rapper. He wants his art to honor his Lakota roots.

Starr Chief Eagle

The hoop dance is special for the Sioux. Dancers use hoops to make different shapes with their bodies. The hoop's circle represents the circle of life. Starr Chief Eagle is a world-famous Lakota hoop dancer. She travels around the country to teach hoop dancing to others.

Once, bison provided the Sioux with food, clothing, shelter, and tools. Bison meat was carefully cut and dried to preserve it.

The Sioux believe that food is sacred because it gives life. Long ago, the Sioux hunted animals and gathered wild foods on the prairie. They traded with other tribes who grew crops. They ate meat, wild rice, corn, wild potatoes, and berries.

One popular Sioux dish is wohanpi soup. Traditionally, it is made from bison, wild turnips, and wild potatoes. Sioux people still enjoy it at celebrations and gatherings.

Culture Close-Up

Sean Sherman is known as "the Sioux chef." The famous Lakota chef cooks with ingredients that are native to North America, such as bison, wild rice, and wild plants.

SIOUX CELEBRATIONS

One of the biggest celebrations for Sioux people is the wacipi, or **powwow**. In the Dakota language, the word *wacipi* means "they dance." A wacipi lasts for several days. People sing, dance, play games, and celebrate their culture.

The Black Hills Powwow happens each October in Rapid City, South Dakota. Events include a fashion show, parade, and competitions for dancers, singers, and drummers.

Sweat lodge ceremonies are also important for the Sioux. The Lakota practice the *inípi*, which means "to live again." A low lodge is built from young trees and covered in hides. People sit inside around heated rocks.

During the ceremony, people pray and sing. The lodge heats up, and people get sweaty. They leave with a feeling of energy and rebirth.

Culture Close-Up

The Sun Dance is the most sacred religious ceremony for the Sioux people. It involves four days of special rituals. The ceremony is not usually open to outsiders.

During the Sun Dance, people dance around a pole made from a tree trunk.

FAMOUS FACES

There are many famous Sioux people. Zitkála-Šá, or Red Bird, was a Dakota writer who fought for voting rights for women and Indigenous people in the early 1900s.

Frank Waln is a Lakota musician who mixes traditional music with hip-hop. He uses his songs to speak up for Sioux people.

Basketball great Kyrie Irving was given the name "Little Mountain" by the Standing Rock Sioux. His mother was born into the tribe.

LESSONS FROM THE SIOUX

The Sioux believe that all living things share a special bond. They believe that the land is a source of strength. They continue to fight for ownership of their sacred lands in the Black Hills.

Sioux people celebrate their culture and honor their **heritage**. Their stories and traditions can teach all Americans important lessons about living in harmony with nature.

GLOSSARY

conservation (kahn-sur-VAY-shuhn): the protection of valuable things, including wildlife and natural resources

dialect (DYE-uh-lekt): a form of a language spoken by a group of people

heritage (HER-i-tij): traditions and beliefs that people consider to be an important part of their history

hides (hides): animal skins that are used to make leather

Indigenous (in-DI-juh-nuhs): the earliest known inhabitants of a place

reservations (rez-ur-VAY-shuhnz): areas of land set aside by the government for ownership by an Indigenous American tribe

sacred (SAY-krid): holy, very important, and deserving of great respect

settlers (SET-luhrz): people who make their homes in a new place and who have historically invaded and oppressed Indigenous peoples who originally lived there

tepees (TEE-pees): tents that are shaped like cones and made from animal skins; traditional homes of Sioux people

powwow (POU-wou): a gathering of Indigenous Americans that is organized for social or ceremonial reasons and that may include traditional singing, dancing, and drumming

FACT CHECK

1. The Lakota, Dakota, and Nakota are all ________.

   A. sacred places   B. ceremonies   C. Sioux people

2. Long ago, the Sioux hunted ________.

   A. horses   B. bison   C. eagles

3. A wacipi is ________.

   A. a celebration   B. a food   C. a weapon

4. Crazy Horse was a Sioux ________.

   A. dance   B. leader   C. battle

Answers: 1. C, 2. B, 3. A, 4. B

FURTHER READING

Locke, Kevin. *The Seventh Direction: A Legend of Creation.* Medicine Wheel Publishing, 2024.

Nelson, S.D. *Grandma's Tipi: A Present-Day Lakota Story.* Harry N. Abrams, 2023.

Speidel, Sage. *Waci! Dance!* Red Deer Press, 2024.

ON THE INTERNET

Minnesota Historical Society: Explore the Seven Council Fires
www.mnhs.org/sevencouncilfires
Explore a digital archive of artifacts from Dakota, Lakota, and Nakota tribes.

National Park Service: Wind Cave National Park
www.nps.gov/wica/learn/index.htm
Learn more about the park and explore podcasts, video clips, photographs, and more.

Native American Hall of Fame
nativehalloffame.org
Find biographies of well-known Native Americans from the 1860s to the present.

INDEX

ABOUT THE AUTHOR

Anne Accardi is an author from Kansas City, Missouri. She is thrilled to share facts about Indigenous Americans with young people. She loves history and finding ways to connect the past with the present and future. When she's not reading or writing, you can find Anne in a library, museum, or movie theater.